BIRTHDAYS
in Different Places

Lauren McNiven & Crystal Sikkens

Crabtree Publishing Company
www.crabtreebooks.com

Learning About Our GLOBAL COMMUNITY

Authors: Lauren McNiven and Crystal Sikkens

Publishing plan research and development:
Reagan Miller

Substantive editor: Crystal Sikkens

Editor: Reagan Miller

Notes to educators: Shannon Welbourn

Proofreader and indexer: Janine Deschenes

Design: Samara Parent

Photo research: Crystal Sikkens

Production coordinator and prepress technician: Samara Parent

Print coordinator: Margaret Amy Salter

Photographs:
Alamy: © Agencja Fotograficzna Caro: pp5 (top left), 13 (top);
    © Israel images: pp5 (bottom right), 7; © Richard Rickard: p8;
    © Bon Appetit: p14; © AA World Travel Library: p16

iStock: © Aldo Murillo: title page; © ziggy_mars: Table of Contents;
    © Cimmerian: pp5 (top center)

Shuttestock: © ChameleonsEye : front cover, p18; © Ragne Kabanova: pp 4 (top right), 19;
    © Somjin Klong-ugkara: p21 (top); © think4photop: p21 (bottom)

Superstock: Travel Pix Collection / Jon Arnold Images: pp5 (top right), 9; Cultura Limited p17

All other images by Shutterstock

Front cover: A family celebrates a boy's Bar Mitzvah at the Western Wall (or Wailing Wall) in Israel.

Contents page: Shichi-Go-San ("Seven-Five-Three") is a traditional celebration in Japan for children ages three, five, and seven. It is celebrated every year on November 15.

Library and Archives Canada Cataloguing in Publication

McNiven, Lauren, author
        Birthdays in different places / Lauren McNiven, Crystal Sikkens.

(Learning about our global community)
Includes index.
Issued in print and electronic formats.
ISBN 978-0-7787-2011-9 (bound).--ISBN 978-0-7787-2017-1 (paperback).--
ISBN 978-1-4271-1652-9 (pdf). ISBN 978-1-4271-1646-8 (html)

        1. Birthdays--Juvenile literature. I. Title.

GT2430.M36 2015   j394.2   C2015-903947-9
                                                            C2015-903948-7

Library of Congress Cataloging-in-Publication Data

Names: McNiven, Lauren, author. | Sikkens, Crystal, author.
Title: Birthdays in different places / Lauren McNiven, Crystal Sikkens.
Description: New York : Crabtree Publishing Company, [2016] | Series:
    Learning about our global community | Includes index.
Identifiers: LCCN 2015032413 | ISBN 9780778720119 (reinforced library binding
    : alk. paper) | ISBN 9780778720171 (pbk. : alk. paper) | ISBN
    9781427116529 (electronic pdf : alk. paper) | ISBN 9781427116468
    (electronic html : alk. paper)
Subjects: LCSH: Birthdays--Cross-cultural studies--Juvenile literature.
Classification: LCC GT2430 .M46 2016 | DDC 394.2--dc23
LC record available at http://lccn.loc.gov/2015032413

Crabtree Publishing Company

www.crabtreebooks.com   1-800-387-7650

Printed in Canada/112015/EF20150911

Published in Canada
Crabtree Publishing
616 Welland Ave.
St. Catharines, Ontario
L2M 5V6

Published in the United States
Crabtree Publishing
PMB 59051
350 Fifth Avenue, 59th Floor
New York, New York 10118

Published in the United Kingdom
Crabtree Publishing
Maritime House
Basin Road North, Hove
BN41 1WR

Published in Australia
Crabtree Publishing
3 Charles Street
Coburg North
VIC 3058

Contents

Our Global Community

Did you know that you share Earth with more than seven billion people? All these people live in different countries around the world. Each country is made up of many small **communities**. A community is a group of people that live, work, and play in the same area. Everyone on Earth also belongs to one huge community—the global community.

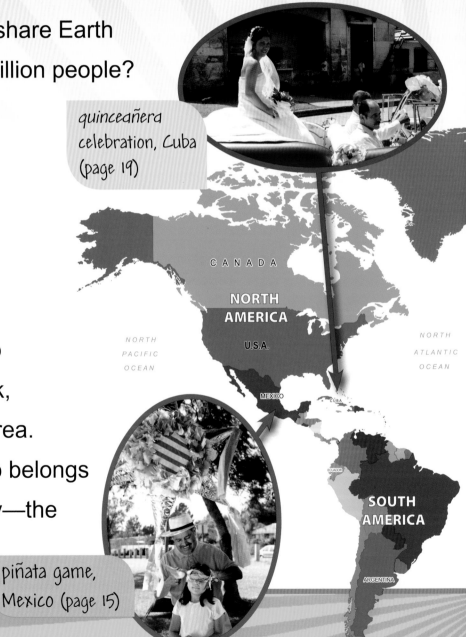

quinceañera celebration, Cuba (page 19)

piñata game, Mexico (page 15)

Different and alike

Finding out how people in our global community live helps us understand how we are all the same in some ways. It also teaches us about the special things that make us **unique**, or different.

Everyone in the world has a birthday! This is one way we are all alike. In this book you will learn how people in different areas of the world celebrate birthdays. Some of these places are shown on the map below.

birthday pie, Russia (page 11)

birthday wreath Germany, (page 13)

third, fifth, and seventh birthday festival, Japan (page 9)

fried plantain birthday dessert, Ghana (page 10)

lifting the birthday person in a chair, Israel, (page 7)

ASIA

RUSSIA

EUROPE

GERMANY

FRANCE

ITALY

GREECE

EGYPT

AFRICA

GHANA

NIGERIA

ETHIOPIA

INDIA

NEPAL

CHINA

JAPAN

CAMBODIA

PHILIPPINES

AUSTRALIA

SOUTH ATLANTIC OCEAN

Everyone Has a Birthday!

A birthday is a celebration that happens once a year on the day a person was born. Each person shares their birthday with around 18 million other people on Earth. Many people celebrate their birthdays in similar ways. Other birthday celebrations are very different around the world.

Decorations, food, and games are part of many birthday celebrations.

Birthday traditions

Some birthday celebrations are based on **traditions**. Traditions are customs, or ways of doing things, that have been passed down from adults to children. The special ways you and your family celebrate birthdays are family traditions. A tradition in Israel involves the birthday boy or girl wearing a crown made from leaves or flowers and sitting in a decorated chair. Guests then dance around the chair and sing.

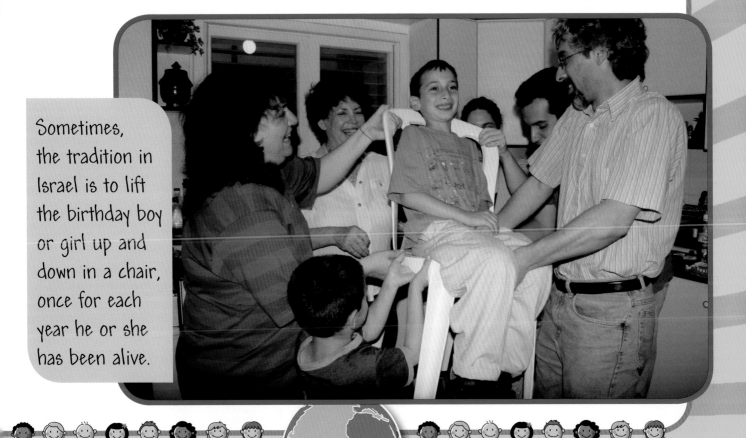

Sometimes, the tradition in Israel is to lift the birthday boy or girl up and down in a chair, once for each year he or she has been alive.

Cultural Traditions

The ways people celebrate special events such as birthdays are often part of **culture**. Culture is a way of life shared by a group of people. Culture includes things such as food, language, clothing, and **religion**. Different cultures have their own birthday traditions or customs.

In Cambodia, followers of the religion of **Buddhism** receive a birthday blessing from a **holy** man known as a monk.

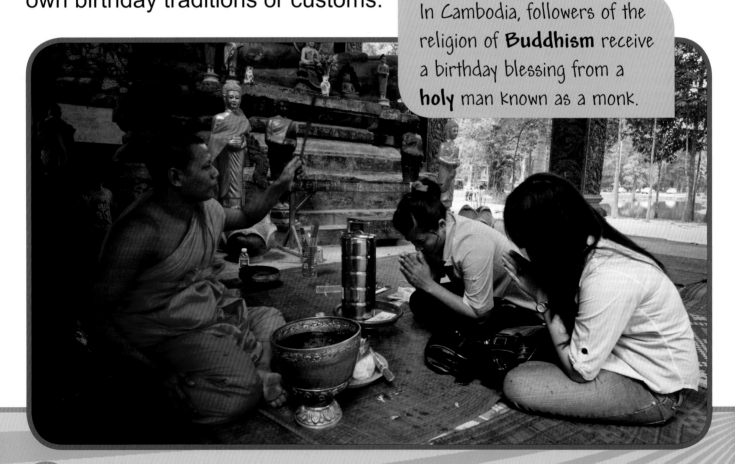

Birthday clothes

Some people celebrate their birthday in special clothing. In India, many children wear colorful clothing to school on their birthday and hand out special chocolates to their classmates. In Ghana, some people wear white clothing when they attend their birthday dinner with family and friends.

In Japan, a special festival celebrates children that are turning 3, 5, or 7. During this festival., children dress in their finest clothes or traditional **kimonos**.

9

Food

Food is an important part of many birthday celebrations. Many people in Ghana wake up to a special breakfast made from sweet potato and egg on their birthday. Children and adults in Sweden start their birthday with a special breakfast in bed. People in China eat long noodles on their birthdays. The long noodles represent, or stand for, a long life.

Fried plantain chunks is a popular birthday dessert in Ghana. Plantains are similar to bananas.

Birthday cakes

A birthday cake is a special dessert served in many places around the world. Birthday cakes come in different sizes, shapes, and flavors. Some cakes are made from fruit, and others are made of ice cream. Some cakes in Britain or Canada even have prizes such as coins baked in the center. Many cakes are topped with lit candles that represent the age of the birthday person. It is the birthday person's job to blow them all out in one breath.

In Russia, people eat a birthday pie instead of a cake. A birthday greeting is carved into the crust.

Birthdays in Sweden are often celebrated with princess cakes. These layered sponge cakes are topped with smooth, green icing and a pink rose.

Birthday Decorations

Have you ever seen balloons tied outside a house where a party is taking place? Balloons are a common birthday decoration in the United States and many other places! Paper streamers, banners, and party hats are other popular items used to decorate for someone's birthday.

Birthday decorations often have bright colors.

Different decorations

Other places have their own special decorations for birthday celebrations. Birthday parties in Egypt are beautifully decorated with fruit and flowers. These decorations represent life and growth. In the Philippines, blinking lights are strung outside the birthday person's home. In Germany, a wooden wreath is an important birthday decoration. Each year, up until a child turns 12, a new candle is placed in the wreath and lit.

The German birthday wreath also includes a "life candle." This large candle is lit every year for good luck.

Birthday Games

Games are often part of birthday celebrations. In Nigeria, many children play a birthday game called "Pass the Parcel." The parcel is a gift wrapped in layers of paper. Children sit in a circle and pass the parcel around while music is played. When the music stops, the person holding the parcel unwraps a layer of paper. The person that unwraps the last layer gets to keep the gift inside.

Children in Russia play a birthday game where they are blindfolded and must pick a prize off a clothesline.

Container of treats

In Mexico, **piñatas** are used in a popular birthday game. A piñata is a decorated container filled with candies and small toys. It hangs down from a string, and children try to hit the piñata with a stick while wearing a blindfold. Once the piñata breaks open, the treats spill onto the floor for the guests to collect.

Piñatas are made in many different shapes and sizes.

Name Day

In many places, celebrating your name day is a bigger event than celebrating your birthday. In the **Christian** religion, it is a tradition that each day of the year is dedicated to a particular saint, or holy person. A person's name day is celebrated on the day dedicated to the saint he or she is named after.

Name day celebrations in Greece often include a visit to a church dedicated to your name-day saint. Visitors light a candle and give an offering, or small gift of money.

In Italy, name day is known as *onomastico*. Lots of food, including cake, is served on a person's *onomastico*.

Modern celebrations

In some places, the name day tradition has changed slightly. More names have been assigned to each day of the year. In other places, people no longer celebrate a saint on their name day, but they still throw a big party. Guests often come to the home of the person to give them their best wishes. Some guests might also bring a small gift.

Coming-of-age Birthdays

In some cultures, certain birthdays represent coming-of-age. This is when a child begins to be viewed as an adult. Many religions have special **ceremonies** on these important birthdays. Followers of the **Jewish** religion celebrate with a Bar Mitzvah when a boy turns 13, and a Bat Mitzvah when a girl turns 12.

Many Jewish people live in Jerusalem, Israel. Bar and Bat Mitzvahs often take place at a holy site known as the Western Wall.

In many places, such as Cuba, girls wear headpieces, called tiaras, and long, white or pink dresses to their *quinceañeras*.

Quinceañeras

In some countries, a coming-of-age birthday for a girl is age 15. On this birthday, she celebrates her *quinceañera*. People that follow the Christian religion begin the event with a religious ceremony. Afterward, a large party with dancing, food, and gifts follows. Some *quinceañeras* include a "changing of the shoes" ceremony. In this custom, the girl's father helps her put on her first pair of high heel shoes. This ceremony represents that she has become a woman.

New Traditions

Many people that follow the religion of **Islam** celebrate a child's birth by giving gifts to the poor. This is becoming a custom in other cultures as well. Instead of receiving gifts for their birthday, people might ask guests to donate, or give, money to a **charity**. A charity is an organization that helps people or animals in need.

Donation box

n box

Guests at your birthday party could also donate food, clothing, or toys to be given to others in your community.

Helping others

Some people might use their birthday party to support areas of the world that are in need of help. In 2015, an **earthquake** shook the country of Nepal. It damaged buildings and took the lives of over 9,000 people. Help is needed to rebuild hundreds of thousands of homes and buildings. Using your birthday party to raise money for a cause such as this is a great way to help others in our global community.

Money donated by people around the world helps supply the people of Nepal with food and clean drinking water.

Notes to Educators

Objective:

This title encourages readers to make global connections by understanding that even though people around the world have different birthday customs and traditions, every one of us has a birthday, and family and friends usually gather to honor us on our birthday.

Main Concepts Include:

- birthday celebrations are often based on cultural traditions passed down through generations in the family
- celebrations often mark important ages in growing up

Discussion Prompts:

- Revisit the various cultural traditions and customs surrounding birthday celebrations from around the world. Ask readers how they are the same and how they are different from how their family celebrates birthdays. They can create a Venn diagram to help with their comparison.

Activity Suggestions:

- Invite children to write a story and draw pictures, or create a scrapbook of pictures from one of their own birthday celebrations. Add captions to explain what is going on.
- Encourage children to add details about food, decorations, clothing, and anything else that is important to the way they celebrate their birthday.
- Invite each child to present their birthday scrapbook or story to the class.
- Guide students by providing questions for them to answer such as:
  - Who is in each picture?
  - What is happening in each picture?
  - How did people prepare for the birthday celebration?
  - What food and games were at your birthday?
- Encourage children to point out their favorite parts of the birthday celebration and whether they are part of an old or new tradition.

Books

Landford, Mary D. *Birthdays Around the World*. HarperCollins, 2002.

Glassman, Jackie. *Birthdays Around the World*. Benchmark Education Company, 2010.

Walker, Robert. *Happy Birthday!* Crabtree Publishing Company, 2011.

Websites

www.theholidayspot.com/birthday/traditions/.
Discover how kids around the world mark their birthdays with traditions and games from different cultures.

http://holidayyear.com/birthdays/
Find out which famous people around the world have the same birthday as you.

www.kidsparties.com/TraditionsInDifferentCountries.htm
Readers will enjoy this list of entertaining birthday customs from around the world.

Glossary

Note: Some **boldfaced** words are defined where they appear in the book.

Buddhism [BOO-diz-uh m] (noun) A religion based on the teachings of Buddha

ceremonies [SER-uh-moh-nee s] (noun) The official activities or events that happen on an important day

Christian [KRIS-chuh n] (adjective) To do with Christianity, a religion based on the teachings of Jesus Christ

earthquake [URTH-kweyk] (noun) When the Earth shakes or trembles

holy [HOH-lee] (adjective) Describing a person or thing dedicated to God

Islam [is-LAHM] (noun) A religion based on the teachings of Muhammad

Jewish [JOO-ish] (adjective) To do with Judaism, a very old religion that follows one God

kimono [kuh-MOH-noh] (noun) A loose robe traditionally worn in Japan

religion [ri-LIJ-uh n] (noun) A set of beliefs and values that is followed and worshipped by people

Index

A noun is a person, place, or thing. An adjective tells us what something is like.